Programme of Mr W.S. Woodin's New Entertainment ... the Olio of Oddities

by W S. Woodin

PROGRAMME
OF MR
W.S. WOODIN'S
NEW
ENTERTAINMENT
FOR A THOUSAND NIGHTS
A LIST OF ODDITIES
INCLUDING
A LOOK
LAKES
PRICE-SIXPENC
SKETCH BOOK
CAR BAG
OLIO OF ODDITIES
THE OLIO OF
ODDITIES.

POLYGRAPHIC HALL,

KING WILLIAM STREET, CHARING CROSS.

MR.

W. S. WOODIN'S

OLIO OF ODDITIES,

AN ENTIRELY NEW AND ORIGINAL

MIMICAL, MUSICAL, PICTORIAL, POLYGRAPHIC, AND PANORAMIC

ENTERTAINMENT.

PROFUSELY ILLUSTRATED BY

SKETCHES OF CHARACTER,

AND CHARACTERISTIC SKETCHES OF THE

SCENERY OF THE LAKE DISTRICT

OF

LANCASHIRE, WESTMORELAND, AND CUMBERLAND

(TAKEN FROM THE SPOT),

WITH DIORAMIC VIEWS OF THE MOUNTAINS, LAKES, AND WATERFALLS
OF THIS ROMANTIC REGION OF ENGLAND.

Dress Stalls, - 3s.   Area Seats, - 2s.   Amphitheatre, - 1s.
Private Boxes,   -   One Guinea.

JOHN K. CHAPMAN AND COMPANY, STEAM MACHINE PRINTERS, 5, SHOE LANE, AND PETERBOROUGH COURT, FLEET STREET.

PROGRAMME.

Part First.

Induction and Introduction, Respective and Retrospective—The Opening of a Cabinet of Curiosities—Advertising, its Publicity and Eccentricity, a Streetological Sketch, being a Picture from the Pavement—Illustrations of Human Nature, from a well-known work, bound in boards—A Review, with an Extract.

Embodiment — AN ANIMATED SANDWICH.

Reminiscences of the Past, and Influences of the Present—"Nothing, if not Critical"— Reviewers Reviewed, and Critics Criticised.

VOCAL ILLUSTRATION—"A CHAPTER OF CRITICS"

(Ancient, Modern, Musical, Artistic, and Dramatic),

Dr. JOHNSON, Mr. VIVIAN VIVID, Mr. VANDYKE BROWN, VISITOR IN BOXES, OLD PLAYGOER IN PIT, "ONE OF THE PUBLIC" IN THE GALLERY.

Trite Topics Treated Tolerably—A Glimpse of London in Season and out of Town—Where to go and whither—A Moving Situation and a Fixed Resolve—A Morning Call and its Consequences—Hints for Incidents Supplied Incessantly.

Impersonation — SIR HARRY HINTON.

"Off for the North," an Orthodox Movement—The Poppletons at the Lakes—An example to follow—Our Native Land—A Home Tour and a Broad Hint.

VOCAL ILLUSTRATION—"TRAVELLING AND TRAVELLERS."

LEAF ONE FROM THE SKETCH BOOK,

KENDAL, FROM THE CASTLE.

Liabilities of Locomotion—Tickets Taken—Collections and Re-Collections.

Daguerreotype — MR. THEOPHILUS TRAMROAD.

Speculative Philosophy—A Curious Train of Thought—Steam Ingenuity.

LEAF TWO FROM THE SKETCH BOOK,

WINDERMERE, FROM THE FERRY.

4

Wayside Whims and Roadside Rambles —— A Countryman and his Colloquy.

Daguerreotype—GILES JOSKYN.

LEAF THREE FROM THE SKETCH BOOK,

LOWER RYDAL FALL.

Eccentricity of Character —— Rules and Regulations —— The Country Squire.

Impersonation—SQUIRE CLUTTERBUCK.

LEAF FOUR FROM THE SKETCH BOOK,

THE SLATE QUARRY.

A Page from the Past—Admired Antiquity and Desirable Novelty—Something that has never been thought of before—The Proof Given.

Impersonation—LADY ESTHER EVERGREEN.

LEAF FIVE FROM THE SKETCH BOOK,

WINDERMERE, ESTHWAITE, AND CONISTON.

VOCAL ILLUSTRATION—"MODERN CHANGES."

The Route Continued, and what springs therefrom—An Odd Companion—Dates and Dinners —A Peculiar System of Gastronomic Mnemonics—Realities of Every-Day Life, and a Gentleman with an Artificial Memory.

LEAVES SIX AND SEVEN FROM THE SKETCH BOOK,

ESKDALE IN A STORM, & PICTURESQUE MILL BY THE ROADSIDE.

Daguerreotype—MR. GUSTAVUS GABBLETON.

Reasons and Recipes—Discourse on Dietetics, with a Table of Contents—Advice to "Young Persons about to Marry"—How to Dress Hare.

LEAVES EIGHT AND NINE FROM THE SKETCH BOOK,

KESWICK & BASSENTHWAITE. DERWENTWATER & BASSENTHWAITE

Visit to an Evening Party—Notes on Newspapers.

Impersonation—MISS CLARA CHATTAWAY.

VOCAL ILLUSTRATION—"METROPOLITAN GOSSIP."

FROM OUR OWN (FAIR) CORRESPONDENT.

LEAF TEN FROM THE SKETCH BOOK,

BARROW FALL.

Part Second.

More Introductions : Social, Civic, Comprehensive, Concise, and Unsolicited—Mr. Tilbury Twitters, Mrs. Pompous, Mr. Finch Lane, of Cornhill, and Itinerant Street Cutler—Public Speaking : its Phases, Phrases, Points, and Peculiarities.

VOCAL ILLUSTRATION—"PUBLIC SPEAKERS."

With Daguerreotype Sketches of Mr. Crosby Hall, M.P. for Rattleborough; Mr. Sergeant Fluster, Counseller for the Plaintiff; and Mr. Felix Flummer.

LEAF ELEVEN FROM THE SKETCH BOOK,

ULLESWATER.

Guide to the Lake District—A Model after the Antique—An Old Acquaintance—A *Cicerone* on Hire, and his Legendary Lore.

Impersonation — GAFFER GRAINGER.

LEAF TWELVE FROM THE SKETCH BOOK,

THE CASTLE ROCK IN THE VALLEY OF ST. JOHN.

Mutability and Instability—An instance of both—Sketching a Sketcher.

Impersonation — MR. WAVERLEY VACIL.

LEAF THIRTEEN FROM THE SKETCH BOOK,

THE DRUID'S CIRCLE.

Meetings and Greetings—Recognitions of the Road—Hibernian Humour and Naval Narratives—A Story without an End.

Impersonation—Capt. CALLAGHAN CARMICHAEL O'CULLENDER.

LEAF FOURTEEN FROM THE SKETCH BOOK,

BORROWDALE (BY SUNSET)

A Difference of Opinion, with the Relative Results—Diffidence and Confidence, with Accidents and Incidents—A Certain Cure for Nervousness.

Impersonation — MR. CYMON SENSITIVE.

VOCAL ILLUSTRATION—"THE SUPPER PARTY."

With Daguerreotype Sketches of the Hon. Mr. Chevy Chase; Mr. Percy Vere, the Punster; Mr. Jonathan Clencher, of New York; and Mr. McMonney, of Glasgow.

LEAF FIFTEEN FROM THE SKETCH BOOK,

ULLESWATER (BY MOONLIGHT)

Music and Moonbeams—Songs and Starlight—A German Tourist.

Impersonation — HERR OTTO, OF ROSENBERG.

VOCAL ILLUSTRATION—"GERMAN SONG."

LEAF SIXTEEN FROM THE SKETCH BOOK,

COTTAGES NEAR CARLISLE.

Homeward Bound—Ladies' Maids and their Accompaniments

Impersonation — MADEMOISELLE THERESE.

LEAF SEVENTEEN FROM THE SKETCH BOOK,

CARLISLE.

VOCAL ILLUSTRATION—"LA BELLE THERESA."

LEAF EIGHTEEN FROM THE SKETCH BOOK,

THE METROPOLIS.

FINALE—"LONDON BY DAYLIGHT AND GASLIGHT,"

A Myriographical, Musical, Mimical, and Pantomimical Comic Census of the Inhabitants, with Daguerreotype Sketches of Street Salesmen and Evening Entertainers.

EXPLANATORY PROGRAMME.

THE LAKE SCENERY.

1.—KENDAL, FROM THE CASTLE.

KENDAL, the largest town in Westmoreland, is prettily situated in a valley on the banks of the river Ken or Kent. The woollen manufacture was founded here as early as the four-teenth century by some Flemish weavers, who were invited by Edward III. to establish themselves and their trade in this locality. With the poets of the seventeenth century the excellence of this cloth was a frequent theme of admiration. The bold outlaws of Sherwood appear to have been especial patrons of the Flemish looms, and Falstaff's knaves, in Kendal Green, will long perpetuate the reputation of the cloth, and that of the minions of the moon who wore it. The town still maintains its manufacturing character; and serges, druggets, and worsted yarn, give employment to a considerable number of the inhabitants. On the east of the town, forming a conspicuous object, as the traveller approaches by the railway, are the remains of Kendal Castle, occupying the summit of a tolerably steep eminence, once the abode of the Barons of Kendal, and still more recently associated with history as the birth-place of Catherine Parr, the last wife of Henry VIII.; it is now a ruin, with only four broken towers and the vestiges of the outer wall to show its by-gone importance. Seen from this elevation, the course of the railway, the town itself, the valley, with the sparkling river winding through it, and the undulating hills beyond, which remind the spectator of his being on the verge of a mountainous district, all supply a succession of tempting landscapes. On the western side of the tower, opposite the castle, is Castle How Hill, the base of which is circled by a deep fosse, and which is presumed to have been the spot where the last penalty of the law was formerly exacted. An obelisk was placed here, in 1778, to commemorate the revolution of the century before.

II.—WINDERMERE FROM THE FERRY.

THE tourist who is fortunate enough to enter Bowness on a bright sunny summer morning, and to arrive at the Lake of Windermere at a time when the steam yacht is just departing, will find in the lively aspect of the little pier, the miniature craft, floating hither and thither along the banks, and the troops of joyous, happy-looking excursionists, that are thronging to this picturesque region, ample proof that the encroachment of the railway has not marred its fascinations, by extending the sphere of their enjoyment. Windermere is about eleven miles long, running nearly north and south, and in one place is above a mile wide, but its average width is not more than two-fifths of a mile. Its greatest depth, opposite Ecclesrigg Crag, is forty fathoms, or 240 feet. Its principal feeders are the rivers Brathay, and Rotha, which unite about half a mile before they fall into the lake; but there are numerous tributaries, besides streams from Troutbeck, Esthwaite Water, and Blenham Tarn, that flow into the lake at different points of its course, until it finally escapes by the Leven into the Irish Sea, at Morecambe Bay. Curwen's Island, or Belle Isle, nearly opposite Bowness, offers a very agreeable point for a brief excursion to those who cannot spare the time for making a complete circuit of the Lake. The walk belting the Island is skirted by noble trees; the oak, luxuriant with the growth of centuries, the feathery birch, the tall larch, the weeping willow, and the graceful ash yielding every gradation of tint and colour that a lover of woodland beauty could admire.

By means of the Ferry, the lake can be crossed at this point for a trifling charge.

III.—LOWER RYDAL FALL

THE Village of Rydal is one mile and a half from Ambleside. What is called Upper Rydal Fall, is a little more than fifty feet high, dashing first in a narrow stream down a precipitous rock, and then expanding into a wide sheet of water, as it flows into a rocky basin beneath. The Lower Fall is a cascade of smaller dimensions, but possessing a miniature beauty of its own which cannot fail to excite admiration. The effect is materially heightened by the way in which it is usually presented to the eye of the spectator. You enter an old summer house, in the grounds of Rydal Hall, and the removal of a shutter reveals the glittering Waterfall in all its artistic prettiness, as it glides down a rather precipitous cleft in a black rock, and foams up again in a thousand prismatic ripples, beneath an old grey bridge, which, with its covering of ivy, seems to have spanned the Waterfall with the sole purpose of increasing its landscape beauty. A peasant, seen above the arch, or a waggon crossing with its load of hay or corn, gives that animation to the scene which is really required, not only to add to its general dioramic effect, but to convince us, by the introduction of animated objects, that the scene represented to us by nature is not a cleverly-devised illusion of the painter. Not far from this Fall is the Cottage on Rydal Mount, rendered hallowed ground to all lovers of poetry by having been, for thirty-seven years, the residence of Wordsworth, and the place where the poet died, April 23rd, 1850, sixteen days after he had completed his 80th year.

IV.—SLATE QUARRY.

For miles around this district the mountains are grouped in massive combinations of striking grandeur, throwing up their lofty summits in vast shadowy outlines, till the imagination may convert them into the semblance of gigantic billows, tossed up by the storms of the deluge, and petrified in their upward course. At this spot some extensive excavations for slate have been carried on. The place goes by the local appellation of the White Moss Quarry.

V.—WINDERMERE, ESTHWAITE, AND CONISTON.

We have here one of those extensive prospects that so often delight the tourist in his progress. The scenery hence to the shores of Windermere will be found replete with pastoral beauty. Esthwaite Lake is two miles in length, and one-third of a mile in breadth. A peninsula swells from the western shore, and pleasantly relieves the monotonous regularity of the margin. Beyond are the Lake and Vale of Coniston, hemmed in by magnificent mountains, and disclosing a view that breaks upon the eye with almost theatrical surprise.

VI.—ESKDALE.

This beautiful Valley is watered by the Esk, which, after a course of about sixteen miles, enters the sea near Ravenglass. The Vale is narrow at the spot where it is entered, but it widens rapidly towards the west. It contains two or three hamlets and a few scattered houses; great numbers of sheep are pastured in it. The encircling mountains are the Seathwaite Fells on the left, and projections from Scawfell on the right. The scene is here beheld under the aspect of one of those sudden storms that occasionally overtake the traveller.

VII.—MILL ON THE ROAD TO KESWICK.

THE view from this spot is singularly pleasing. There is a fine breadth of cultivated land, sprinkled with hamlets and solitary houses, amongst which the Mill, here represented, forms a picturesque object.

VIII.—KESWICK AND BASSENTHWAITE.

WERE there no other charms in the lake districts than those concentrated in the first views of Keswick, the tourist would yet feel that his pilgrimage hitherto had not passed without reward. The Lake of Bassenthwaite is rather narrower than the rest, being only one mile broad, with a length of four miles, and a depth of seventy-two feet. The three miles that separate it from the north end of Derwentwater, consist of low meadows, often flooded in wet weather, but in fine weather resplendent with the blossoms of the heather and the gorse. Dewars' Family Hotel commands a fine view of Derwentwater; and the tourist may there meet with every comfort and accommodation, at reasonable charges.

IX.—DERWENTWATER.

A SCENE of more luxuriant beauty than this lake presents can hardly be imagined. It extends in an oval form, about three miles from north to south, and is about a mile and a half broad. From the transparency of the water, pebbles being seen twenty or fifteen feet beneath the surface, it reflects, as in a mirror, the amphitheatre of mountains surrounding it, and many a white cottage or woody glen, that lies upon its bright green banks, finds its image reflected with a flattering brilliancy of colour in the smooth waters beneath. The lake, at irregular intervals of a few years, exhibits the singular phenomenon in the rising of a piece of ground, called the floating island, from the bottom to the surface of the waters. It is composed of a loose mass of vegetation, which rises to the top when the decay of its material has yielded the necessary gas to sustain its buoyancy. As soon as the gaseous vapour is exhausted, it again descends. Its appearance is rare enough to render the floating island an object of much interest, and the newspapers record its presence amongst us with all the paragraph honours due to the visit of a distinguished stranger. In the present sketch, the Lake of Bassenthwaite is also shown from a different point of view.

X.—BARROW FALL.

TWO miles from Keswick is Barrow House, at the back of which is Barrow Fall, the cascade here represented. It is 124 feet in height, and forms a charming object in the surrounding landscape. Behind it branches off the road to Watendlath, a little hamlet situated in a most secluded valley.

XI.—ULLESWATER.

THIS lake is of a serpentine shape, nine miles long, a mile wide, and about 200 feet in extreme depth. It is divided by promontories into three sections, called reaches, of unequal size, the smallest being the highest and the largest the middle reach. Four small islands adorn the uppermost—the scenery around which is of the grandest description. The view here presented shows some of its most picturesque features. The cliffs here, vast and broken, rise immediately from the stream, and often shoot their masses over it, whilst the glassy depths below mirror back their overhanging projections.

XII.—CASTLE ROCK.

A SHORT distance on the Keswick side of Threlkeld, the road leading into the vale of St. John branches off on the right; the rock here depicted, and which has given celebrity to the valley, stands near the extremity on the left. Its resemblance to a fortification is very striking. It is the scene of Sir Walter Scott's "Bridal of Triermain," and the poet has sketched it in verse after his own happy fashion, as it is supposed to have presented itself to the charmed senses of King Arthur.

XIII.—THE DRUID'S CIRCLE.

WE have here a prodigious enclosure of great antiquity, formed by a collection of stones on the top of a gently sloping hill. This *area*, about 300 yards in circumference, besides being surrounded by the mound of pebble stones, has a large block of unhewn stone, nearly twelve feet in height, placed in the centre. This is supposed to mark the scene of Druidical judicature. By sunset, these vestiges of a remote age assume a singularly romantic and striking appearance.

XIV. BORROWDALE.

AT Borrowdale, such a scene of romantic grandeur is unfolded, that the tourist may fancy he has encountered a spot which has the shattered fabric of a primeval world, which has not yet had its tremendous scars effaced. The valley is six miles in length, and the disposition of mountains and crags, the tumbling together of steeps and slopes, precipices and promontories, woods, ravines, and isolated summits, combine to form a series of landscapes of the most attractive beauty.

XV.—ULLESWATER BY MOONLIGHT.

THE lake tourist will find, if he can contrive to have a moonlight sail upon the lake, the recollection of it imperishable. The most imaginative of poetic dreamers can fancy nothing more delightful than to enjoy an excursion of this kind, floating amidst the beauties of Ulleswater, and poised for awhile between two worlds of stars. Music is generally and advantageously employed to enhance the effect.

XVI.—COTTAGES AT CARLISLE.

THE traveller who leaves the ancient city of Carlisle by a night train, will, doubtless, well remember the picturesque cluster of cottages here represented. Homeward bound, the panorama hence conducts the tourist back to the metropolis, where we leave him with the suggestion, that those who become first acquainted with the myriad beauties of their own country, will, at least, be afterwards best entitled to pursue their pilgrimage after beautiful scenery, in a calmer and more satisfactory spirit of just appreciation.

XVII.—TERMINUS AT CARLISLE

XVIII.—THE TRAIN AT NIGHT.

XIX.—TERMINUS OF THE NORTH WESTERN RAILWAY, EUSTON SQUARE.

XX.—THE GREAT METROPOLIS, UNDER THE ASPECT OF DAYLIGHT AND GASLIGHT.

OPINIONS OF THE PRESS.

THE TIMES, May 14.

The new room which Mr. W. S. Woodin opened on Saturday bore every sign of established prosperity. It is situated in King William-street, Charing-cross, and has hitherto not been especially celebrated, but Mr. Woodin lifted it from obscurity by his own name, and the word "Woodin," written in gas above the door, marked out the house among less distinguished edifices. On entering, the visitor found himself in the presence of spacious stalls, clad in rich crimson velvet, and requiring that their occupants should be in full dress, an area in which the exigencies were less severe, and a row of handsome private boxes. Let us add, that if he arrived after 8 o'clock he found all these places *full*, and might deem himself fortunate if he were allowed to stand by the door. The stage is even more striking than the *salle*, apparently supported, as it is, by craggy rocks, and decorated with rich hangings. Altogether, the whole thing denoted that Mr. Woodin was sure of his position, and could afford to construct, paint, and decorate for himself on a more costly scale than he had ventured on heretofore.

However, not only was the room new, but Mr. Woodin inaugurated it by a new entertainment, entitled the *Olio of Oddities*. His old entertainment, called the *Carpet Bag and Sketch Book*, was, it may be remembered, in itself somewhat flimsy fare, and, though by his talent for impersonation and the quickness of his transformations he raised it to a popularity which few amusements of the sort have attained, we could constantly feel that all his salt was required to give flavour to so much insipidity. The lecturer, in fact, perpetually triumphed over his lecture. But the *Olio of Oddities* is a very different affair. It is smartly written throughout, and the types of character introduced are by no means of that hackneyed kind that looks like a perpetual reproduction of one of the late Mr. Mathews's old "At Home" books. Moreover, the variety of personages introduced is exceedingly great, and this the author has attained, not by extending the entertainment, but by removing every character from the scene as soon as its peculiarities are developed, and never pausing on an exhausted pleasantry. While Mr. Woodin is provided with better material to work upon, he also displays great improvement on his own part. His former delineations were seldom more than amusing sketches, but his best characters in the new entertainment are highly-coloured portraitures, rendered the more remarkable by the shortness of the time during which each remains before the public eye. In the course of one song entitled a "Chapter of Critics," Mr. Woodin ducks his head under the table at intervals of about a minute in length, and after each duck rises as a new figure. First, he is a veritable portrait of Dr. Johnson, with dress, stomach, and voice, all complete; then he is a slim, fashionable connoisseur of music, with large whiskers and eloquent shrugs; next he rises with a red beard and an Anglo-foreign aspect, to discourse technically on pictorial art; afterwards he is an occupant of some dress circle, who thinks Shakspeare "slow" and adores the *ballet*; in another second, he is an old connoisseur of the pit, who mumbles over the palmy days of the drama; and lastly, he is a visitor to the one-shilling gallery, proud to patronize his favourite actor, quick to recognize a friend among the audience, and determined to enjoy everything. We did not test these personages by Sterne's stop-watch, but we shall not go far wrong in stating that they were all—the aggregate all—represented, both as to dress and characteristic peculiarity, in less than 10 minutes, and that the mechanical dexterity of the changes, admirable as it was, was the least meritorious part of the achievement. The traditional figure of Dr. Johnson and the nervous excitement of the London *gamin*, intoxicated not by ardent liquor, but by an overpouring sense of felicity, indicate a profound conception of character and a power of accurate delineation that are perfectly marvellous, when we take into consideration the number of directions in which they are employed, with scarcely a moments interval. These "Critics" are all half-length figures acted behind a table, but Mr. Woodin also introduces several completely-dressed figures, who step to the front of the stage, and excite wondering inquiry how they could have got their clothes on, and how Mr. Woodin, who has just been talking in his own (remarkably fashionable) coat and continuations, has so completely changed his age, dimension, and sex—one or all, as the case may be—that not a vestige of his former nature is visible to the eye. The ladies of such entertainments are generally rather caricaturish, and unwittingly betray a masculine foundation, but Miss Clare Chattaway, who is Mr. Woodin's chief heroine, is the complete *belle* of a modern room. The full dress, the ringlets, the smalltalk, the affected laugh, the manner in which she arranges herself at the piano, are all perfect.

We are not going through the long list of Mr. Woodin's personages, partly because it *is* a long list (including something like 50 changes), partly because we do not wish to destroy the charm of novelty to the future patrons of his performance. The *Olio of Oddities* is rendered perhaps the best characteristic monologue ever presented to a public.

MORNING HERALD, May 14.

WOODIN'S OLIO OF ODDITIES.—Mr. W. S. Woodin, whose entertainment, called the *Carpet Bag*, was, in its amount of success, only inferior, to that of Mr. Albert Smith's *Mont Blanc*, has been occupying himself of late in the preparation of another, which, inherently superior to that in which his first attempt as a delineator of "character" was made, promises to be among the most popular of its class that we have had. He has removed, too, to new quarters, and has converted that mysterious building in King William-street, which has been exposed to such strange vicissitudes of occupation—moral, immoral, literary, vocal, and admonitory—into a commodious theatre, decorated very prettily, and christened the "Polygraphic Hall." Here has he pitched his tent, and here he opens out his *Olio of Oddities*, the first glimpse of which he gave us on Saturday night.

We have repeatedly taken occasion to allude to the extraordinary facilities possessed by Mr. Woodin in the embodiment of those eccentric personages behind a table which were originated by the elder Mathews and Frederick Yates. But neither of these illustrious mimics demonstrated such a profuse repertory of "sketches" upon a single evening as this gentleman, who dives his head into a box, and comes up somebody else every five minutes; besides emerging occasionally in an elaborate full length, without regard to sex. The *Carpet Bag* was productive of a numerous assortment of these odd creations, but the *Olio* presents us with some where about fifty—a gallery of changes unprecedently large. The pretence that suggests the new entertainment is at our through the lake districts; and Mr. Woodin not only depicts the "characters" he affects to have met with, but exhibits in connection with them, views of the scenery. But we do not only have the tourist and the native. Divers extraneous personages are pressed into the songs, which constitute such an important feature in the contents of the *Olio*. A chapter on Critics furnishes us with a series of portraitures, the idea of which is as novel as the execution is remarkable. Dr. Johnson in the wig, immortalized by Sir Joshua Reynolds, propounds his full-bellied sentences, while, in rich antithesis, Mr. Vivan Vivid and Mr. Vandyke Brown, let off a round each of æsthetical jargon about music and painting. Then we have the languid fop in the private box; the burly despiser of modern innovations in the pit; and the costless god, as vociferate with his tongue as with his hands, in the gallery. It will scarcely be believed that these separate individualities are introduced into *one* song, and that with a rapidity of mutation which no professor of the arts of transmogrification ever excelled. In another song, the pertinacious M.P., the voluble pleader in a breach of marriage case, and the after-dinner orator of a bridal party, are delineated with the same sort of extempore effect. But one of the completest sketches brought in in this way is the tipsy fox-hunter, whose soddened eye, unsteady arm, and inarticulate speech, while proposing the toast of "the ladies," provoke peals of laughter. The full length figures are all more or less good—the Cumberland squire who lives, walks, and eats scrupulously by rule; the drawing-room belle, who simpers a song of gossip akin to the famous "Galignani's Messenger" of Albert Smith; the old country lady who is puzzled at modern fashions; and the German minstrel,

being, perhaps, the best. Among the half portraits, the inveterate smell-feast, Mr. Gustavus Gabbleton, the sweep, and the policeman, are the most graphic.

The entertainment went off on Saturday evening with immense spirit and success. The hall was crowded; and Mr. Woodin may reckon upon his *Olio of Oddities* being in great vogue for many nights to come. It well deserves any measure of patronage that may be bestowed upon it.

MORNING ADVERTISER, May 14, 1855.

MR. WOODIN'S ENTERTAINMENT.—After seven hundred and sixty-two performances of his *Carpet-Bag and Sketch-Book*, and a lengthened tour in the provinces, Mr. Woodin has resumed his place amongst the London exhibitions, and on Saturday might initiated an entirely new entertainment, entitled an *Olio of Oddities*, which is very justly described as novel, original, mimical, musical, pictorial, and panoramic. Notwithstanding the talent exhibited in his former entertainment, and the extraordinary popularity it attained, we think the present far superior, both in conception and execution. The characters are drawn more directly from the life, are more typical of existing foibles and fashions, and are more briefly and pointedly illustrated. There is just enough and no more of each. The idea is firmly conceived and sharply outlined, is illustrated by a smart joke, or a characteristic anecdote, and *hey presto!* the embodiment has evaporated, and the lecturer, with his point device every-day dress, and gentlemanly tone, is before you, merely to introduce you to another oddity who advances from the folds of the hangings that serve as walls to the room, or springs up from a table placed on either side of the stage.

If there were no other talent exemplified in this entertainment then that shown in the rapid chanes, and the clever "make up" of each character, it would be well worth seeing as a marvel of dexterity. Costuming has become quite an art, and the characteristic wigs and dresses show an amount of humorous observation that really brings the maker of them into the category of an artist. The instantaneous manner in which they are donn'd and doff'd exceeds anything we have yet seen; and it may be imagined what it is, when we find that fifty dress characters have been exhibited, several comic songs sung, and a great deal of monologue uttered by one individual, in the course of two hours and a half. Mr. Woodin's ease and rapidity in this manner are something wonderful; and we must add, that practice has greatly improved his acting and his elocution. Though all is as rapid as an arrow, it is equally smooth and sure. There is no bustle through the swiftest execution, and he has so much mastered his art that there appears in parts even a leisurely grace, that adds a considerable charm to the performance.

What may be termed the libretto is exceedingly well composed; the songs run glibly, and are set to pleasing tunes, and sparkle with unexpected puns and pointed allusions. They are judicious in length, and in no instance trenched on the patience of the audience; but, on the contrary, came rapidly to a climax, and left off whilst a full relish still existed in the audience for them. The character gallery has, on the whole, been very well selected, though it appears to us to have a mixed set. One portion, and that far of the highest kind, consists of sketches made from the life; such as the varieties of musical and dramatic critics; the modern fox-hunter, a young gent, who proposes a health at a modern dinner, the costume of which is itself an excellent piece of comedy; and *Mr. Theophilus Tramroad*, a railroad official, who lectures on a very large subject in a very little room. These are verities of the time, and are particular to the age, and bring the impersonator into the category of an author and a satirist. The other set are of a more general class. *Giles Joskin, Squire Clutterbuck, Lady Evergreen*, and even *Miss Chattaway* are well known to us. They are acted and dressed to perfection, and especially the last, so that they are very effective. Mr. Woodin excels in his female characters, which, in such representations, are generally coarse exaggerations, but, in his performance, are dramatic creations. *Lady Evergreen* never forgets she is a lady of the old school, and *Miss Chattaway's* appearance really created a sensation amongst the audience, who could scarcely believe in the identity of the enactor.

The Gallery in King William-street, Charing-cross, has been fitted up appropriately, and named Polygrapic Hall. The entertainment is illustrated by a number of dioramic views of the lake scenery, the supposed place of action; and the proscenium has been decorated in accordance with this idea. These views make an agreeable back ground for the eye to rest upon during the brief intervals that occur between the changes. A pianoforte accompanies the songs; but by no means forms a prominent part of the entertainment. It is scarcely necessary, after the account we have given of this performance, to say it was triumphantly successful; and that it deserves, and bids fair, to outrival in popularity even the former entertainment of Mr. W. S. Woodin.

DAILY NEWS, May 14.

WOODIN'S OLIO OF ODDITIES.—Mr. W. S. Woodin having, in the course of 762 representations almost worn out his "Carpet Bag and Sketch Book," has finally shut both up, and opened in their stead a new comic entertainment entitled "The Olio of Oddities," principally the result of a tour in the romantic district of the lakes in the north of England, from which he has brought back much of its beautiful scenery, and portraits of many of its inhabitants. This new entertainment was given for the first time on Saturday, at the King William-street Rooms. Charing-cross (now elevated to the dignity of "The Polygraphic Hall"), and may be briefly described in the words of a very competent authority, "the bill," as being "mimical, metrical, musical, pictorial, and poly-

graphic," which means that Mr. Woodin effects fifty rapid metamorphoses of voice, character, and costume, sings some eight or ten songs, and adds to the whole an excellently painted moving panorama of the romantic region before alluded to. But few men can play in their time more parts, and fewer still play them so well as Mr. Woodin; and his entertainment will, doubtless, become as successful as its popular predecessor. The audience on Saturday was too large for the " hall."

MORNING POST, May 29.

WOODIN'S ENTERTAINMENT.—Mr. Woodin, already so favourably known to the public by his "Sketch Book" and "Carpet Bag," at the Regent Street Gallery, has started a fresh "concern," in King William Street, Strand. This new entertainment he has named "Woodin's Olio of Oddities." It takes a more ambitious range than Mr. Woodin's previous performances. It comprises an entirely new comic entertainment, and a moving panorama of the romantic lake scenery of England. This new speculation of Mr Woodin's is a decided "hit," and one that seems to be highly appreciated by the public.

SUNDAY TIMES, May 12.

MR. W. S. WOODIN.—Although, after the long and successful "run" of the *Carpet-Bag and Sketch-Book*, the public may fancy that they have attained a tolerably correct estimate of the versatile talents of Mr. Woodin; we can emphatically assure them that, until they have seen his new entertainment, they know nothing whatever of the extent of his abilities. The *Olio of Oddities*, as it is called, is not only far more sparkling, but also far more substantial than its predecessor, and his delineations of character have about them a robust individuality, that show higher qualities than mere rapidity in effecting changes, or the knack of clever imitation.

The entertainment is supposed to be based on Mr. Woodin's reminiscences of a recent tour to the English lakes, and a number of picturesque views pass along the back of his stage as he acts or sings in front. These views, however, are rather intended to amuse the spectators during the intervals of the performance, and though the characters described are, for the most part, encountered in the course of the northern excursion, Mr. Woodin by no means confines himself to any particular locality. Almost at the commencement, he sings an excellent song, entitled "A Chapter of Critics," in which, to make an exhibition of various critics, old and modern, he successively transforms himself, both in manner and person, into Dr. Johnson (!), a foppish *connoisseur* of music, a bearded judge of painting, an exquisite tenant of the boxes, a growling occupant of the pit, and an excitable *habitué* of the gallery. One song alone suffices to make him five different personages, to both ear and eye, and each one of them is as distinct as possible from the other. An old country squire, who does everything by method, and an old lady, dressed in the genteelest fashion, who marvels at modern changes, are exquisite comedy sketches; especially the latter, who, in a song, characteristic of her sentiments, expresses her estimate of new fashions in a tone of the most delicate sarcasm. A fat blustering gentleman, who reveres nothing that he cannot eat, and recollects persons and places by the dishes with which they are associated in his memory, is another excellent conception, and he is coloured with all unctuousness by Mr. Woodin. But the most marvellous character of all is Miss Clara Chattaway, a real young lady to all appearance, in a full ball dress and flowing ringlets, who seats herself at the piano with the most feminine airs, and with a voice equally feminine, sings a song about "Metropolitan Gossip," that is capable of as close adaptation to the topics of the day as the "Galignani's Messenger" of Mr. Albert Smith. The lovely Clara concludes the first part of the entertainment, and so very brilliant is she, that it is somewhat difficult to prevent an anti-climax in the second. Among the most effective characters, we would mention the Member of Parliament, the barrister for the plaintiff in a breach of promise case, and the vendor of scissors, in the song entitled "Public Speakers," and (best of all) a drunken fox-hunter, who proposes the toast of "The ladies" after supper, and to assume whose character, Mr. Woodin must assuredly have put another head on his shoulders.

The audience last night completely crowded the new room, which is divided into pit, stalls, and boxes, and is fitted up with the most luxurious elegance.

ILLUSTRATED LONDON NEWS, May 19.

MR. W. S. WOODIN'S OLIO OF ODDITIES.—This entertainment commenced on Saturday last, in the Polygraphic Hall, King William Street, Charing Cross, which has been elegantly fitted up for the purpose. In rapidity and brilliancy, as well as in the number of characters, this entertainment is almost unique The whole, too, is so artistically disposed—every point is so well introduced, and all the parts follow in such exact order, that Mr. Woodin receives as much support from the medium in which he works as the materials themselves require of illustration from his various talents. The action of the entertainment consists of a Visit to the Lakes, and the *dramatis personæ* are composed of such individuals as the tourist would be likely to meet with on such an excursion. These are accompanied with a diorama of the scenery, which has been beautifully painted. Eighteen scenes are thus very effectively exhibited: among which are Kendal, Windermere, Rydal Fall, the Slate Quarry, Eskdale in a Storm, Keswick, Ullswater, Borrowdale, and Carlisle. The impersonations have been in general well adapted to Mr. Woodin's light and graceful style, which much resembles that of Mr. C. Mathews, and is, in some cases, quite equal to its prototype. Mr. Woodin is a dashing member of the "fast" school; and, in the patter and clatter class of song, is excellent. His best specimen of this sort of thing occurred in "A Chapter of Critics," which commenced with a capital portrait of Dr. Johnson, as a con-

trast to more modern professors of the "art deteriorative," and concluded with a Murillo Sketch of a boy in the gallery of a theatre, enthusiastically animated and embodied to the life. Sir Harry Hinton, Mr. Theophilus Tramroad, and Squire Clutterbuck are the full-length portraits in the first part; but the little bit of Giles Joskyn chaffing the Londoner, may be regarded as most effective. There are, also, a grand "impersonation" of Lady Esther Evergreen, with a song; and what is called a "daguerreotype" of Mr. Gustavus Gabbleton, with a technical memory referable to the *cuisine*, that have proofs of vitality. In the second part, our memory dwells on Mr. Cymon Sensitive, and the gorgeous appearance of Miss Clara Chattaway—the make-up of the latter being astonishing. The concluding character is that of Clown, in proper costume, imitating the Senor Perea Nena; with which piece of exaggeration Mr. Woodin brought down his curtain to the unanimous applause of a crowded house.

BUILDER, May 26.

AN ARTISTIC OLIO.—As the upholders of art, in whatever shape it appear, so as it be genuine, we feel we should scarcely fulfil our conditions, still less satisfy our inclinations, did we not devote a few lines of approbation to Mr. Woodin's "Olio of Oddities." Mr. Woodin is no common artist; his sketches are neither the startling crudities of ultra-originality, nor a series of *rifacimenti* of well-known portraits, touched up and redressed to suit modern tastes; but there is a freshness of conception and vigour of execution about them which indicate undoubted ability, and effectually disarm the slightest suspicion of plagiarism. Apart from the individual merits, more or less, of the numerous portraitures which constitute the structure of this very entertaining monologue, the number of the characters and extreme rapidity of their changes are something quite marvellous to witness. In the space of two hours, he presents you with 30 or 40 portraits, all drawn from the life, and some of them so true to their originals that the most obstinate stickler for likeness cannot fail to recognise their strong resemblance to the type whence they are derived. The first character, "An Animated Sandwich," makes his audience as completely "at home" as himself, and proves his touch to be masterly; and his subsequent impersonations more and more illustrate the value of first impressions. A piece of comic vocalisation introduces a "Chapter of Critics," from the sententious and ponderous Dr. Johnson to the off-hand, fragmentary, ejaculatory critics of the shilling gallery. "Travelling and Travellers" next introduce you to Mr. Woodin's Sketch-book, a series of well-painted views of the Lakes of Cumberland. Evidence of good taste pervades the whole arrangements. The stage is separated from the audience by a refreshing mass of green rock-work, lit by coloured lamps, and the fittings are very elegant. It is, as we said before, an artistic exhibition, and as such we warmly recommend it to the patrons of art in general.

CPSIA information can be obtained
at www.ICGtesting.com
Printed in the USA
BVHW040105130819
555665BV00021B/3153/P